ADAMSVILLE/COLLIER HEIGHTS

INDIA

the people

Bobbie Kalman

A Bobbie Kalman Book

The Lands, Peoples, and Cultures Series

 Crabtree Publishing Company

www.crabtreebooks.com

The Lands, Peoples, and Cultures Series

Created by Bobbie Kalman

to my parents, Janet and Paul Lewis, who inspired me to discover India

Written by
Bobbie Kalman

Coordinating editor
Ellen Rodger

Editor
Jane Lewis

Editors/first edition
Christine Arthurs
Margaret Hoogeveen

Production coordinator
Rose Gowsell

Contributing editor
Lisa Gurusinghe

Production
Arlene Arch

Separations and film
Embassy Graphics

Printer
Worzalla Publishing Company

Photographs
Chris Beeman: p. 17 (bottom right); G. Boutin/Photo Researchers: p. 21 (right); Ian Clifford/E-Side Studios: p. 16, 26; Betty Crowell: p. 14; Ken Faris: p. 25, 31 (top); Jacquie Gilbey/Ken Hood: p. 5 (bottom); Catriona Gordon: p. 30; George Holton/Photo Researchers: p. 27 (bottom); Susan Hughes: p. 15 (both), 23 (bottom); Jefkin/Elnekave Photography: p. 11 (top left), 12 (bottom); Wolfgang Kaehler: p. 18, 19 (bottom); Sudha & Abdullah Khandwani: p. 4; Noboru Komine/ Photo Researchers: p. 19 (top); Daniel Lainé/Corbis: p. 11 (bottom); Jane Lewis: p. 3; Eric Melis: p. 31 (bottom); Shawn Mulvenna: p. 13; Porterfield/ Chickering/Photo Researchers: p. 20; Carl Purcell: p. 7, 10, 19 (middle); David Samuel Robbins/Corbis: p. 21 (left); Larry Rossignol: p. 22; Jeffrey L. Rotman/ Corbis: p. 24 (top); Pamela Sayne: p. 28; Jeff Sample: p. 23 (top); Ron Schroeder: p. 24 (bottom), 27 (top); Mike Silver: p. 17 (top and bottom left); Erika Stone/ Photo Researchers: p. 29; Tony Stone Worldwide/ Masterfile: p. 6; Ingrid Mårn Wood: p. 5 (top), 11 (top right), 12 (top), 24 (middle); X. Zimbardo/ Hoaqui/Photo Researchers: cover; Daniel Zirinsky/ Photo Researchers: title page.

Every effort has been made to obtain the appropriate credit and full copyright clearance for all images in this book. Any oversights or omissions will be corrected in future editions.

Illustrations
Dianne Eastman: icons
Renée Mansfield: p. 8-9
David Wysotski, Allure Illustrations: back cover

Cover: A young Indian woman wears elaborate and intricate gold jewelry.

Title page: Over a billion people live in India. These colorfully dressed citizens live in the northwestern state of Rajasthan.

Back cover: The elephant has been an important part of India's culture and history for centuries.

Published by
Crabtree Publishing Company

PMB 16A	612 Welland Avenue	73 Lime Walk
350 Fifth Avenue	St. Catharines	Headington
Suite 3308	Ontario, Canada	Oxford OX3 7AD
New York	L2M 5V6	United Kingdom
N.Y. 10118		

Cataloging in Publication Data

Kalman, Bobbie, 1947
    India, the people / Bobbie Kalman. – Rev. ed.
    p.cm. – (The lands, peoples, and cultures series)
Includes index.
    ISBN 0-7787-9382-6 (RLB) -- ISBN 0-7787-9750-3 (pbk.)
    1. India–Juvenile literature. [1. India.] I. Title. II Series.
DS407 .K27 2001
954–dc21   00-055586
                                                                    LC

Contents

India is a large Asian country with the second-highest population in the world. Over one billion citizens have a history that dates back thousands of years. Some of these people are **Hindu**, others **Muslim**; some work, others go to school; some speak Gujarati, others Tamil. Despite the great variety of lifestyles and customs, Indians try to accept the differences among their various groups in order to live together peacefully.

Although the people of India are part of an ancient **culture**, the independent country of India is young. Its government is working to build a nation that will provide all its citizens with food, shelter, education, and employment. For any country, these needs are difficult to meet. India is burdened with a tremendous population and many serious challenges.

India's citizens follow different religions, speak countless languages, wear different types of clothing, and practice a variety of different customs and traditions. Together, they make India unique.

Indian **civilization** may be as old as 10,000 years. It began in a valley along the Indus River, from which India gets its name. The Indus Valley is in the northwest, in what is now Pakistan. The ancient civilization flourished for thousands of years. In 1500 B.C., people began to move away from the Indus Valley. Historians and **archeologists** are still working to find out why this occurred. It may have been an environmental disaster, such as a flood or an earthquake, that caused the population to spread eastward across northern India and into the south.

Emperor Ashoka

Over its long history, India has been invaded by many foreigners, and ruled by emperors, *rajas*, *shahs*, and *sultans*. The nation was first united for a time in the fourth century B.C. during the Mauryan Empire. At that time Emperor Ashoka converted to **Buddhism**, a religion opposed to killing. He became a kind-hearted leader who encouraged people of different faiths to live together peacefully.

Today, the many-spoked wheel of Ashoka is the symbol that appears on India's national flag. Just as the numerous spokes join together in the center to make a wheel, the different groups of people come together to form the country and culture of India.

Princely states

Throughout most of its early history, India consisted of several states, each one ruled by a *raja*, or prince. *Rajas* were rich men who were the heads of powerful families. When one family ruled a large area and became very powerful, it was called a dynasty. The golden age of Indian art and science occurred in the fourth and fifth centuries during the Gupta dynasty.

The City Palace in Jaipur gives visitors a glimpse of a time when powerful Indian princes ruled India.

The Muslim empires

In the year 712, Muslim warriors invaded India's northwestern borders. They wanted to spread the Islamic faith, a new religion that originated in the Arab countries. Despite many invasions and battles, the Muslims did not fully take control until 500 years later. A number of Muslim dynasties called the Delhi Sultanate then ruled northern India. The last Sultan of Delhi was defeated in 1526 by Muslims from Afghanistan. These conquerors formed the Mogul Empire, which ruled for about two hundred years. Its leaders were called *shahs*.

European traders

Vasco da Gama of Portugal was the first European to reach India. After he arrived in 1498, the Portuguese, Dutch, French, and British came to trade with India. These countries craved India's spices, textiles, and other luxury items. For years they fought India and one another for trading privileges. A British company called the East India Company was the most successful trader and controlled most of India for many years.

The British Raj

Eventually India was made a colony of the British Empire in 1858. India became a unified country under British rule. Railways and roads were built; postal and telegraph services were set up. The British Raj (*raj* means "rule") governed India without the consent of the Indian people. Being governed by foreigners made the Indians unhappy. They did not have the same rights or privileges as the British, nor were they allowed a say in how their country was run. Britain used India's **raw materials**, such as cotton, to make manufactured goods in its own factories. These goods were then sold back to the Indians. Producing goods in Britain increased Britain's wealth and prevented the growth of industry in India.

(below) The British built many buildings during the Raj. Many examples of British architecture can be found throughout India. This building is a train station in Mumbai.

For many centuries India was ruled by foreign powers. At the beginning of the twentieth century the people of India acquired a renewed pride in their **heritage** and a desire to be independent from Britain. Mohandas Karamchand Gandhi, a great leader, helped make this dream a reality. Gandhi believed that Britain had no right to rule India. He felt that Indians should govern their own country. The Indian people respected Gandhi's wise words and honored him with the title Mahatma, meaning "Great Soul."

Gandhi's peaceful struggle

Mahatma Gandhi taught that it is right to hate what is unjust but wrong to hate people. In the struggle for independence he did not want anyone to be killed, whether British or Indian. He believed in using non-violent ways to achieve India's goals. He encouraged Indians to refuse to buy British goods, quit British jobs, and start their own businesses. He also organized peaceful protests. Even when Gandhi was jailed for opposing Britain, he remained patiently dedicated to the struggle for independence. Gandhi's steadfast dedication inspired the Indian people to build a new nation.

The salt march

Gandhi's most successful protest was the salt march. For centuries Indians had collected their salt directly from the sea. When the British took over, Indians were charged an unfair tax on salt that was produced in their own country. Gandhi decided to protest by collecting his own salt. The whole world watched as he and thousands of his followers walked twenty-six days to get to the ocean. At the seashore each person collected a handful of salt. This gesture of defiance demonstrated every Indian's desire for freedom.

Independence at last

Gandhi's efforts to bring self-rule to the country he loved were effective. Britain was forced to grant India independence in 1947. Yet not all Indians were happy with the outcome. The Muslim minority was worried about being overpowered by the Hindu majority. The Muslims wanted to form their own country. Gandhi and many others were against breaking up India. After much fighting and bloodshed it was decided that India would have to be divided. Two portions, one in the west and one in the east, were separated from India. Today they are known as Pakistan and Bangladesh.

The first prime minister

Jawaharlal Nehru became India's first prime minister. For many years he had worked closely with Mahatma Gandhi to gain India's independence from Britain. Nehru had a modern outlook, improved India's **economy** by promoting **industrialization**, and promoted women's equality. He worked hard to create a democratic government in the first years of India's independence.

The government of India

The government of India is a **democracy**. In this type of system people elect representatives from political parties. In India these elected representatives become members of **parliament**. Parliament is the governing body that makes the laws. The head of parliament is the prime minister, who is the leader of the political party with the most elected members. He or she chooses officials to help run the government and has the responsibility of carrying out the laws of the land. India also has a president, who is appointed rather than elected.

ॐ The many faces of India ॐ

The Indian population is made up of a whole variety of communities. The people of India may be grouped in many ways: by **race**, religion, language, region, and social position.

India's tribes

The original inhabitants of India are known as Adivasis. There are many different tribes of Adivasis throughout the country. The Adivasis tribes once lived in the forests and tropical jungles. In the twentieth century, many forests were cleared for farming, mining, hydroelectric dams, and other development projects. The Adivasis people have been forced to leave their traditional homes and move to the most remote areas of India.

Today, around seventy million Adivasis are scattered throughout the country. Some live in small, self-contained communities. They hunt and gather food and worship the forces of nature just as their **ancestors** did. They speak their own languages and remain apart from other Indians. Other Adivasis have joined Indian society. Many Adivasis have begun to organize protests against projects that take away their land and resources. Their traditional way of life is in danger of disappearing forever.

Religious groups

People are sometimes grouped according to their religion. The majority of Indians are Hindu. Although Hindus live all over India, practice different customs, and speak different languages, they all follow the Hindu religion. About fourteen percent of India's population is Muslim. Muslims follow a religion called **Islam**. Sikhs, Buddhists, Christians, Jains, Parsis, and Jews make up the rest of the population.

(above, left) This woman belongs to one of the indigenous tribes of India.

(above, right) The majority of Sikhs live in the state of Punjab in northern India. Sikh men do not cut their hair, but wear it up wrapped around their heads in a turban.

(below) This Tamil man marked his forehead for a religious festival.

Many different languages

Language is another way of grouping people. Over thousands of years many languages and **dialects** developed in India. Before modern means of transportation existed, few villagers traveled more than several miles from the place where they were born. As a result, each isolated area developed its own language and customs. Today there are about fifteen officially recognized languages and hundreds of dialects used in India.

The Tamils

Tamil Nadu, which means "the land of the Tamil," is the southernmost state of India. The Tamil people who live there share a strong sense of community. Historically, they were unaffected by Muslim influences in the north. They have therefore been able to hold onto their language and cultural traditions. Most Tamils are Hindu. They have built many magnificent temples, which are fine examples of Hindu art and architecture.

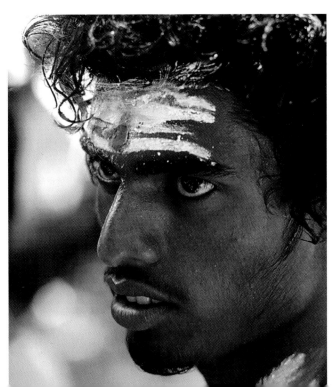

11

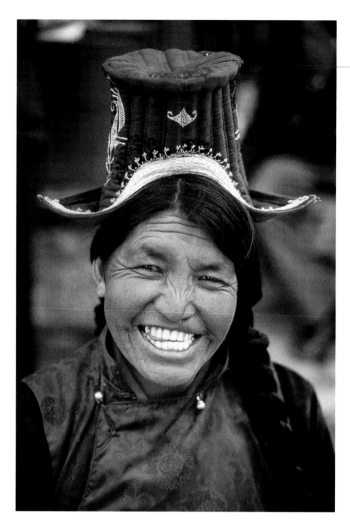

The Kashmiris

The Kashmiris live in picturesque mountain valleys in northern India. Unlike the rest of the country, this area receives snow in winter. Many people in Kashmir live on houseboats on the Jhelum River, which flows through the region. The first houseboats were built because a local law stated that only Kashmiris could own land. Europeans and other Indians who wanted to settle there found a spot on the river and used their boats as homes. Soon this became common among Kashmiris, too.

Many Kashmiris are fruit growers. In winter months they produce beautiful handicrafts. Using willow wood, they weave baskets, lampshades, chairs, and tables. They make carpets from brightly colored threads of wool and cotton. Kashmiris are also well known for their embroidery, jewelry, wood carving, pâpier-maché, and shawls.

Regional differences

Some regions in India are inhabited by distinct groups. Sometimes a whole group of people with already-established customs moved to India and settled in one particular area. For instance, the Parsis fled Persia to live in India. Today most Parsis reside in and around the city of Mumbai.

Sometimes different peoples settled in one area. Over time their customs blended, and new ways emerged. Today these communities have their own distinctive cultures. Many Kashmiris live in the region of Kashmir and have established a unique community. Most Kashmiris are Muslim.

(above) The people who live in the mountainous region of Ladakh have a culture unique in India.

(right) This woman from the Longia Soura tribe in Orissa carries a bundle on her head.

12

The Ladakhi people

Located in the foothills of the Himalayan mountains, Ladakh is one of the highest inhabited places in the world. The people of Ladakh are strong and hardy because they have to survive a cold climate and rugged landscape. The main crop grown by Ladakhi farmers is barley. Shepherds called *changpas* follow their flocks from pasture to pasture. The big, shaggy yak is important to the ancient Ladakhi way of life. Yaks are able to carry heavy loads over the rough mountain terrain. Their long hair is woven into mats and used to make tents called *ribos*. Yaks also provide milk, butter, and meat. Most Ladakhi people are Buddhists.

Division by caste

For thousands of years, Hindu society has been divided into castes, or classes. The **caste system** has four main castes. People in each caste have traditionally followed certain professions. The Brahmin were priests and scholars, the Kshatriya were rulers and soldiers, the Vaishya were landowners and merchants, and the Sudra were **artisans** and servants. People were also divided into thousands of subcastes according to their jobs or positions in life. Over time the caste system became so rigid that people born into a certain caste remained there all their lives. They socialized and married only within their castes. Those who married outside their castes risked losing family and friends.

People followed the caste system because their religion, Hinduism, encouraged them to accept their stations in life. According to Hinduism each person has a *karma* that determines his or her position in society. *Karma* can be defined as fate or destiny. For instance, if you are born a grocer, it is your destiny to remain a grocer as long as you live. *Karma* makes it difficult for you to improve your life by making you feel you should not change it.

(above right) A mother and baby from Jaisalmer in northern India, are dressed for a cold winter morning.

The "children of God"

People outside the caste system were once called "untouchables." These people occupied such a low position in society that other Hindus did not want to come anywhere near them. Untouchables were the poorest members of Indian society and were required to perform the worst jobs.

Mahatma Gandhi campaigned to improve the lives of the untouchables. He gave them the new name Harijan, which means the "children of God." To demonstrate his sincere belief that all people are equal, he took up a broom and began sweeping the streets. No one but the Harijan were ever supposed to do this job. People gathered around him, shocked by his action. No public figure had ever challenged the caste system in this way. Gandhi asked, "How can India be free if all Indians are not free?" Today the Harijan are called Dalits or Scheduled Castes.

Traditions are hard to break

The Indian government has outlawed the caste system because it is unfair. It is trying to make up for the problems caused by the old system. For example, a university education is now possible for many Dalits. Tradition is often hard to break, however, and many people still follow the rules of the caste system.

ॐ Family life ॐ

The traditional Indian family is called a **joint family**. A joint family includes parents, children, aunts, uncles, cousins, and grandparents. In India, three or four **generations** of a joint family may live under one roof! When a couple marries, the woman leaves her home and goes to live with her husband and his parents. Today most Indian families are joint families, although there are also many **nuclear families**.

The all-important marriage

A wedding is an important event in the Indian family because marriage is considered to be the union of two families. Traditionally, parents search for suitable marriage partners for their children from members of their own caste. Partners in arranged marriages often come together as strangers and later grow to love each other. Although most Indian marriages are still arranged, there are also some "love marriages." A love marriage occurs when two people fall in love and then marry each other.

The men of the house

In the typical Indian household the men are in charge of the family and enjoy positions of privilege and respect. The oldest male, usually the grandfather, holds the highest position. All men must earn a living to support their families. Sons inherit the family land or business. The greatest duty of sons is to provide for their parents in their old age.

Women's responsibilities

Women are responsible for looking after the family and household. Taking care of the home is a full-time job, especially for women in rural areas. Village women often begin their day at dawn. They must pound wheat into flour, cook food over an open fire, wash clothes by hand, and carry water from community wells. Besides caring for a husband, children, and parents-in-law, many poorer women also toil in the fields, sell fruit in the market, or work on a construction site.

14

New roles for women

In recent years many women have become professionals who hold jobs outside the home. Women now work as doctors, scientists, engineers, and computer programmers. They hold government jobs and serve in the army. It is often only women from wealthy families who can pursue such careers, but poorer women have also gained more opportunities in recent times. **Union** groups and **cooperatives** have been organized to help women find work, fight against discrimination, and become self-sufficient.

The practice of purdah

In some areas of India, Hindu and Muslim women must remain hidden from other people, especially men and strangers. This practice is known as purdah. When in public, women in purdah wear clothing that covers their entire body, including their head and face. Some of these women rarely go outside their home. For their families, purdah is a sign of honor.

Hope for the children

Children are the center of the Indian household and receive much attention from their loving families. Parents try to educate their children and hope that they will live healthy, happy, and prosperous lives. Many children are now better educated than their parents. If a family is poor, however, children often go to work at a young age to help support the family. India hopes that in the future all children will go to school.

(top) Many families in Jammu and Kashmir live on houseboats. People live on their boats all year long—even in winter when it snows. These boys do not have to go far from home to go fishing!

(bottom) This Kashmiri woman is ready to prepare a tasty fish supper in her houseboat kitchen.

15

There are many different types of homes in India. In urban areas, large extravagant homes surrounded by lush gardens and high walls exist not far from slums full of tiny shacks made from old cardboard and tin. Apartment buildings of all sizes can be found throughout the city. In rural areas, many homes are basic and small.

Village homes

Although sometimes made of bricks or pink sandstone, most village houses are constructed from a mixture of clay, straw, and cow dung. Thick walls help keep out the summer heat. Some homes are built with flat roofs, so family members can sleep on top of their houses in hot weather. Most homes have one or two rooms and perhaps an enclosed courtyard where the animals are kept.

Furniture

The average Indian home has few pieces of furniture. Shelves or storage bins may line a wall, and floor mats provide places for people to sit. An important piece of furniture in many homes is a bed called a *charpoy*. A *charpoy* is a frame with a mat across the top woven out of rope. During the day people sit on it or lean it against a wall. On warm evenings it is taken outside.

The kitchen

In many rural homes, the corner of one room serves as a kitchen area. Food is cooked on a sunken stove or a portable clay stove. Wood or dried cow dung is used as fuel. There are only a few supplies: some pots and pans, utensils, and a flat pan for cooking *chapatis*. Foodstuffs are stored in baskets or brass pots. Often the legs of large bins are set into little bowls of water so that insects cannot climb up the legs and get into the food supply. In larger towns or cities, many houses have a separate kitchen and conveniences such as running water, gas stoves, and refrigerators.

(below) The kitchen floor is kept very clean because cooks traditionally prepare meals on it. This woman and her mother-in-law are making some Indian-style bread.

The family shrine

Essential to the traditional Hindu home is a small space or alcove for a shrine. Here the family keeps a picture or statue of the family's favorite **deity**. The image is frequently washed and decorated with garlands of flowers and incense. Before meals the family makes symbolic offerings of food to the statue. These rituals of worship are called *puja*. Family members pray that their deity will bring them health and good fortune.

(below) Only the wealthy can afford to live in modern suburban neighborhoods such as this one.

(above) Homes vary from region to region. These desert homes are built with bricks made from local materials.

(below) The all-purpose charpoy *is the most essential piece of furniture in the average Indian home.*

17

About three quarters of India's population live in villages scattered across the country. Many of these communities consist of small clusters of houses nestled together, whereas some large villages have hundreds of inhabitants. Generally, families live close to one another and share a strong sense of community with their neighbors. The houses in most villages are built around a square where people can gather. An elected group of elders, called the *panchayat*, meets here from time to time to make decisions concerning village matters. Beyond the village lie the farmers' fields.

Few modern conveniences

The average village home has few **modern conveniences**. Most rural families do not have running water, indoor toilets, washing machines, refrigerators, or air-conditioners. Many families do have television and radio, however. In the past, most villages did not have electricity. Today many do, but it is rarely a reliable supply. **Blackouts** are a common occurrence.

The center of village life

The well is the center of daily life in many Indian villages. It provides water for drinking, cooking, bathing, and cleaning. In some areas well water is also used to water the fields. Water buffalo or oxen are sometimes used to haul the water up from the well. In the past most wells in India were open. In order to fill their jugs, people walked down a few steps right into the water. This made the water dirty and caused sickness to be easily spread. Disease-carrying insects also thrived in open wells. Now most villages have covered wells, which have greatly reduced the spread of disease. Many modern wells also have electric pumps.

Besides being a source of water, the local well is a center of social activity. When villagers go to the well to fetch water or do the laundry, they take the opportunity to visit with neighbors. Friends exchange the latest news and talk about all the things that make life interesting.

Most Indian villages have fewer than one thousand inhabitants.

(left) Laundry is done by hand outdoors and dried in the warm sun.

(below) This young boy is in charge of drying cow dung, which his family will use as fuel for their cooking fire.

(bottom) Many villages do not have running water. Villagers get their water from a community well.

19

ॐ Living in the city ॐ

In India, as in other countries, city streets are busy and noisy places. Not only are they crowded with people, motorcycles, cars, and buses, they also teem with bicycles, **rickshaws**, cows, and street vendors. People rush to get to work. Others beg passersby for a little change. Some do a little shopping. Instead of big department stores, there are small shops, outdoor booths, and merchandise spread out for sale on carpets on the ground. Books, kitchen utensils, medicine, spices, shoes, and a countless number of other items are available in the city streets.

The city also provides many types of entertainment. People often go to the movies or take part in outdoor games and sports. Some families belong to clubs and dine at restaurants. Cities are the cultural centers of India, offering their residents museums, art galleries, historic sights, and theaters.

City problems

Although only twenty-five percent of India's population lives in the cities, urban centers are extremely overcrowded. Each year millions of people flock to the cities to find work, but there are not nearly enough jobs for everyone. There are not enough homes, schools, and hospitals, and not everyone has access to proper toilets or clean drinking water. Traffic jams and accidents are common, and pollution from vehicles and industries has reached dangerous levels.

(above) The streets of India are always filled with people going about their daily business.

(opposite, left) Many older apartment buildings in India have arched balconies like this one.

(opposite, right) These people do not have a place to live, so they sleep on the ground near the railroad tracks.

City apartments

Those fortunate enough to have somewhere to call home often live in small apartments with several relatives. A common type of apartment building is called a *chawl*. A *chawl* has three to six stories, with twenty or more one-room apartments on each floor. There are no separate kitchens or living rooms in these apartments. The tenants on each floor share a bathroom at the end of the hall. Sometimes there is not enough room for the whole family, so some family members sleep on the street. They come home to eat and have their laundry done.

A fortunate middle class

Although many city dwellers are poor, cities are also the home of a growing middle class. Many people who live in cities have good jobs and make a good living. Some families have spent generations in the city, often renting or owning the same home for decades. These families live comfortably with adequate space and facilities. They pay to send their children to private schools and hire servants to help with household chores or to drive the family car. A servant calls every day to pick up the family's dirty laundry. Vendors come right to the door to sell vegetables, spices, or textiles.

City slums

Cities are growing at a fast rate, and this has led to a drastic housing shortage in India. Many city dwellers cannot find or afford accommodation, so they must live in tents or shacks crowded together in slums. Many others sleep on the street. Homeless people can be seen curled up at the sides of buildings and in alleyways on makeshift beds. The people in slums or on the streets do not have toilets or clean drinking water. A large number of the poorest city dwellers originally came from small villages to find employment. Because they can only find low-paying jobs or no jobs at all, they cannot afford to rent apartments or rooms.

21

Sometimes Indians have a hard time understanding one another. From region to region, and sometimes from village to village, people speak different languages or dialects. Areas developed their own languages because villages and towns used to be isolated from one another. In the years before planes, trains, or cars most people passed their whole lives without ever meeting a person from another village.

A common language

Eighteen major languages and over 800 dialects are spoken in India. To help solve communication problems, the government made Hindi the official language of India. Although Hindi is the mother tongue of less than half the population, it is now being taught in every school. Knowledge of the English language also helps bridge the communication gap. English is often used in universities, government, science, and business.

Reading and writing skills

India's **literacy rate**—fifty-two percent—is one of the lowest in the world. Special allowances are made for those who cannot read or write. Many signs use pictures instead of words. Voting cards, for example, use the symbols of the political parties so that people who cannot read are still able to vote. People who are illiterate have a difficult time getting by. It is nearly impossible for them to get jobs other than manual labor. Even finding their way to an unfamiliar place is a challenge for those who cannot read. India is trying to provide everyone with reading and writing skills.

Many village schools have few supplies and poor facilities, but students are eager to learn.

Public and private education

Education is free for all Indian citizens up to age fourteen. Most children attend state schools, which are supervised by the government. Some children attend private schools, which are modeled on British schools. Only parents who can afford to pay the yearly fees can send their children to these schools. Some private schools are run by religious institutions such as Christian missions. Many Indian schools have a uniform, which the students wear every day.

School supplies

In some schools, a slate and chalk are used as learning tools. Unlike paper, a slate can be used again and again. Books are often in short supply. Some schools do not even have desks—students sit on the floor of the classroom. In other schools students sit on benches or chairs and hold their books in their lap.

Work or school?

By law, Indian children aged six to fourteen must attend school. In reality, only about fifty percent attend. In rural areas it is difficult to keep children at school when they are needed to work on the farm. In cities, many children help their parents earn a living instead of going to school. Sometimes girls stay at home to do housework or look after younger brothers and sisters. With so many responsibilities, many children do not finish their schooling.

Going to school

Indian children attend primary and middle school, and some go on to high school. They have final exams at the end of the tenth grade and another set in the twelfth grade to prepare for college or university. To gain entry into university, students must speak, read, and write in English. More than 180 universities, colleges, and technical schools are now open. As a result, more and more students can acquire professions or learn skills and trades. The most popular professions are in medicine, engineering, computers, and agriculture.

(above) **These children live in the city. They get a ride to school on a rickshaw instead of a school bus!**

(below) **When it gets too hot in the classroom, students learn their lessons in the shady schoolyard.**

Occupations

About two thirds of India's people make their living from the land, but there are many other types of jobs in India. Industries and factories employ thousands of people. Some work for the government; others run small businesses of their own. At one time Indians did not have much choice regarding how they could earn a living. Most people worked at the same jobs as those of their fathers. Today, because of better education and new technology, a larger variety of job opportunities is available.

The family business

Many boys are trained by their fathers to carry on the family trade. A farmer's son learns all about the land. A goldsmith's son learns the skill of crafting delicate gold jewelry. A boy may start to help in the family business when he is as young as four or five years old. He works there until his father is ready to retire. Then he takes on the business himself and supports his aging parents. Later on, he teaches his own son the family trade.

India's cottage industries

Indians have always owned and run cottage industries. Cottage industries are small businesses conducted in people's homes. Before India achieved independence, artisans and workers provided goods and services such as jewelry, leather work, blacksmithing, and weaving to the rest of their community.

When India began to industrialize, many cottage-industry owners suffered. People started to buy factory-made goods instead of items made within the community. To counter this trend, Mahatma Gandhi encouraged Indians to start more cottage industries. He hoped that these small businesses would enable people to stay in their villages and create self-sufficient communities. Today the government of India continues to support small businesses. Cottage industries now flourish throughout India.

(top) A doctor treats a patient in a hospital.

(middle) Many passersby stop to have their teeth checked and fixed at this outdoor stall.

(bottom) This stone carver displays his latest work—a large statue of the god Ganesh.

The lure of the city

Many young people leave their villages because there is not enough land for farming or there are too many people employed in the same trades. Some of these people look forward to new lives, whereas others do not want to leave their family and home. Most of them go to the cities looking for work. They soon discover that millions of other people are hoping to find jobs in the city, too. Many of these unemployed people never find jobs. Others end up in low-paying jobs working as rickshaw drivers, household servants, and construction workers.

The bonding bind

Some people end up as bonded laborers. A bonded laborer is someone who works for a money lender in order to pay back a debt. Money lenders pay very low wages and charge their workers large sums of money for the use of equipment and services, including transportation to and from the work site. The employee is forced to continue working because he or she can never save enough money to pay back the original debt.

Bonded labor is now illegal but it continues because many people have never been informed of their rights. Some unscrupulous employers even tell their workers that their debts must be passed on to their children. Millions of people are still trapped in this never-ending cycle of bonded labor and poverty.

A privileged few

University educations and well-paying professional jobs are available to only a small percentage of Indians. It costs a great deal of money to attend university. Professionals such as engineers, scientists, and lawyers often come from privileged backgrounds. The government now has programs that give underprivileged people the chance to attend university and become professionals. As a result, more and more young people will be able to further their education, get better jobs, and improve their living conditions.

In India many people work at manual labor. The workday is long and exhausting, little attention is paid to safety, and employees have no job security.

The Indian government has a great responsibility in the twenty-first century. It must guide the development of India's economy to ensure that all citizens are able to support themselves and their families. To achieve this worthy goal the government has been encouraging industrial development. Unfortunately there are many other social problems that burden the people of India, for which solutions must be found.

The money gap

In India there has always been a huge gap between the very rich and the very poor. Indian princes, whose families once ruled India, possess huge family fortunes. Some merchant families have become wealthy in the business world. These people live in luxury. A middle class has recently emerged due to increased industry. Middle-class families can afford to live fairly comfortable lives. Unfortunately, a much larger number of people have little or no money. With the population of India growing by leaps and bounds, many more people are born into a life of poverty every year. India must do something to close the gap between the rich and poor.

A lack of jobs

A large number of Indians have a difficult time making a living. Many people are unemployed because there are simply not enough jobs for everyone. Others can find work, but not doing what they have been trained to do. These people are underemployed. At one time they studied at college or university, with the hope of entering a career of their choice. They soon discover that the positions they want are already filled. In order to make a living, they accept low-paying jobs. An architect, for instance, might drive a taxi instead of designing buildings because he is desperate for work. These working conditions cause many highly trained people to leave India so they can follow their chosen careers.

(above) Slums have become a part of the landscape in India's cities. People put together makeshift homes of cardboard, tar paper, plastic sheets, or corrugated metal.

The case against caste

For centuries, Indian society was divided into castes. A caste determines a person's place in society and even his or her occupation. Although the caste system has been outlawed by the government, many people still follow its traditional rules. As a result, a person of low caste finds it extremely difficult to improve his or her situation in life.

Women with little say

In traditional Indian society, women have not had the same opportunities as men. While their brothers go off to school, many girls stay home to help their mothers with housework. These girls never learn to read or write and have a hard time getting good jobs when they grow up. Most Indian women work from dawn to dusk to keep their households going. Some work outside the home as well. Although they often have to do the toughest jobs, such as carrying gravel at construction sites, they usually get paid the lowest wages. Because of their low position in society, many Indian women lack power and freedom. Fortunately, this is beginning to change. Women are asking for, and gaining, equal rights and opportunities in all areas of life.

(above) These women work in the tea plantations of northern India.

(below) This homeless man must beg for food or money in order to survive.

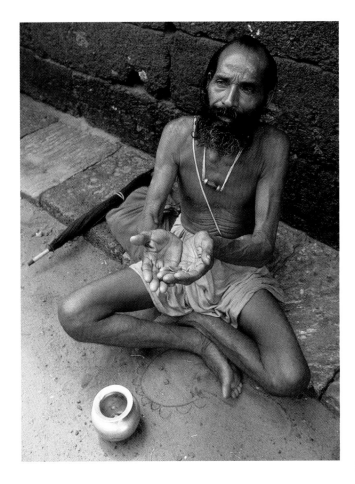

The cycle of poverty

Shanti smiled at her husband, Dipu, who waved to her from his bicycle rickshaw. It was getting late in the afternoon, and Shanti had not yet sold all her lemons. She sat cross-legged at the side of the road, a heap of lemons beside her. Knowing that her boss would be displeased if she did not sell them soon, Shanti called out to the people walking nearby, "Lemons for sale! Good, fresh lemons. Come and get your lemons."

Shanti's throat felt sore from calling out to customers all day long. Just before dawn she had been awakened by the cries of her daughter Devi. Devi needs Shanti's constant attention because she is sick with diarrhea. Shanti came out of the tent to make a little breakfast and tea for Dipu. As she used up the last of the flour to make *chapatis*, she wondered if she would earn enough money by the end of the day to buy food for the family and medicine for Devi.

Shanti got married at the age of sixteen. Before the wedding day, her parents had told her that her future husband would be able to buy her a new house. Her father and mother arranged her marriage to Dipu, a boy from another village. He was the son of a brick maker. Dipu's two older brothers had already entered their father's

business, so Dipu did not have a job. Soon after baby Devi was born, the young couple went to Mumbai to find work and a new place to live.

When Shanti and Dipu reached Mumbai, they marveled at the sights. Dipu noticed all the tall buildings, and Shanti was fascinated by the movie theaters. She imagined how wonderful it would be to work as a ticket seller, but she knew that she was not dressed well enough to apply for a position. The pair did not have enough money to see a movie, but Dipu promised Shanti that someday they would go to the movies together.

The couple had a hard time finding work. Dipu only knew the trade of brick making, and Shanti had only attended school for three years. Dipu finally found a job with a taxi company. While he rides customers around the city on a bicycle rickshaw, Shanti sells lemons on the street for a local farmer. Although they both work, their income is so small that they can barely afford to feed themselves. The young family lives in a tent in the slums of Mumbai.

(above) Despite their poverty, Shanti, Dipu, and Devi enjoy the times they spend together.

An old story

The story of Shanti and Dipu is not a happy one. It is typical of millions of people in India who live without the basic necessities of life. Poor people must struggle to survive with inadequate food, shelter, education, and health care. Like millions of others, Shanti and Dipu are trapped in the cycle of poverty. They earn just enough to get by, but not enough to improve their situation. Higher wages would make it possible for them to save a little money, and low-rent apartments would provide them with a place to live. Better access to education would help Devi get a job when she grows up. These solutions are very difficult to attain.

A discussion on poverty

How is the plight of Shanti and Dipu similar to the plight of poor people all over the world? What are some of the causes of poverty? Why does poverty seem like a circle without an end? Think of at least ten hurdles homeless people must face when they try to better their situations. Why might it be more difficult to break the cycle of poverty in some countries than in others? How can governments help people better their positions in life?

Interview a welfare officer in your city or town, or invite him or her to your school. Learn about the real problems poor families face and why it is difficult for them to improve their situations.

A happy ending?

Write an ending for Shanti and Dipu's story. Have your friends do the same. Do you think Shanti and Dipu would be happy with your endings? Discuss whether your solutions are practical. What do you think the future really holds for this couple and their children? Do you think Shanti and Dipu can be happy even when they are poor? What makes you happy?

(below) This family lives in a tent next to Shanti and Dipu. They came to Mumbai after losing their home in a flood.

ॐ Indian customs ॐ

The colors of India

An ever-present dazzling use of color reflects the atmosphere of India. Houses are often painted pastel pink, blue, or yellow. Multi-colored temples are decorated in great detail. Every market is a kaleidoscope of the luscious colors of fruits, flowers, and bright powdered dyes. Indian fabrics and clothes display every shade of the rainbow. Men wear colorful turbans on their heads. During the festival of *Holi*, everyone is covered in festive powders and dyes. Colors are not only attractive, they are also symbolic. Green stands for youth and life, red for happiness and joy, and blue for peace.

Fortune tellers

For thousands of years Indians have looked to the stars to guide their actions and predict the future. **Astrology** and fortune telling are both part of folk Hinduism. Astrologers are consulted before weddings are arranged and on other special occasions. Fortune tellers set up their wares in the bazaars. Some tell your fortune with the help of a bird!

Guess the Indian words

Many words in the English language were originally Indian words. Here are ten: shampoo, bungalow, tank, thug, pajamas, cashmere, curry, bazaar, jodhpurs, and sandals. Which words belong in each of the following sentences? Write the answers on a piece of paper—not in the book.

1. The __ I use makes my hair squeaky clean.
2. Nico put a new goldfish in his fish __.
3. A __ just grabbed that woman's purse!
4. The jockey on the horse is wearing a hat, a jacket, and a pair of __.
5. My grandmother lives in a __, so she does not have to climb up and down stairs.
6. In winter I wear cozy flannel __.
7. In summer I wear __ so my feet stay cool.
8. My friend Ritu bought a *sari* at a __.
9. Nina made a spicy __ for dinner!
10. I like wearing my soft __ sweater.

Indian people love bright colors. During the Holi *festival they throw these powders at one another, creating an explosion of brilliant colors.*

Holy cow

According to Hindu mythology, Brahmins (priests) and cows were created at the same time. Cows are considered sacred, and dairy products such as milk and ghee (a type of butter) are used in religious ceremonies. It is forbidden by law to kill cows. Every year there is a festival called *Pongal* to honor these holy animals. During *Pongal*, people wash and decorate cows with colorful pastes and flower garlands.

Year-round yoga

Yoga is an example of a daily ritual that grew out of Hinduism. Yoga is used to help maintain a healthy body and mind. Yoga teachers, called yogis, practice yoga as a way of finding peace and spiritual fulfillment. Many people start each day with a series of yoga exercises called "A Salutation to the Sun." They say that doing this makes them feel great the whole day long. Go to your library and find a book on yoga. Try the sun salutation postures. They may make you feel excited about starting the day!

(above) The cow is special to Indian people. Cows are treated with great care.

(below) A yogi greets another new day by saluting the sun at dawn.

Glossary

ancestor A family member from whom a person is descended

archeologist A person who studies ancient cultures by looking at old artifacts and city ruins

artisan A skilled craftsperson

astrology The study of the positions of stars and planets and their influence on people's lives

blackout A period of time during which the supply of electricity is cut off

Buddhism A religion founded by Buddha, an ancient religious leader from India

caste system An ancient Indian social system that classifies people according to birth

civilization A society with a well-established culture that has existed for a long period of time

cooperative An organization owned by all the members, and in which all members profit from the group's work

culture The customs, beliefs, and arts of a distinct group of people

deity A god or goddess

democracy A form of government in which representatives are elected to make decisions for society

dialect A variation of a language

economy The way a country manages its money, goods, and services

generation People born at about the same time. Grandparents, parents, and children make up three generations.

heritage The customs, achievements, and history passed on from earlier generations; tradition

Hindu A follower of Hinduism—an ancient Indian religion based on the holy books called the *Vedas*

indigenous people The first people to live in a certain region or country

industrialization The term used to describe a shift from an agricultural society to one that produces goods in factories

Islam A religion founded by the prophet Muhammad

joint family A family unit in which many members of one family—grandparents, parents, children, grandchildren, aunts, uncles, cousins—live together in one household

literacy rate The number of people in a country or group who can read and write

modern conveniences Up-to-date goods and services that make life easier, such as electricity, running water, refrigerators, and telephones

Muslim A follower of Islam

nuclear family A family unit made up of a mother, father, and children

parliament A group of people that makes the laws for a country

plantation A huge farm that grows cash crops and employs many workers

race A group of people who share similar physical characteristics that are passed along from generation to generation

raw material A substance from the earth that is not yet processed or refined

rickshaw A small, three-wheeled vehicle for one or two passengers

sari The traditional garment worn by many Indian women consisting of a long cloth wrapped around the waist and draped over the shoulder

sultan A Muslim ruler

symbol Something that represents or stands for something else

union A group of people that support one another and work together to achieve certain goals

Index

1 2 3 4 5 6 7 8 9 0 Printed in the USA 0 5 4 3 2 1 0